RYA YOUNG SAILOR

GW01003287

NAME (capitals) ....

ADDRESS ....

....

....

Published by
ROYAL YACHTING ASSOCIATION
RYA House, Romsey Road, Eastleigh, Hampshire SO50 9YA
Tel: 01703 629962   Fax: 01703 629924

Throughout this book the pronouns 'he', 'him' and 'his' have been used inclusively and are intended to apply to both men and women. It is important in sport as elsewhere that women and men should have equal status and equal opportunities.

Cover photograph of a 405 by Peter Bentley
Line drawings by Phil Twining

INTERNATIONAL SAILING LOGBOOK	International Sailing Schools Association
LIVRET INTERNATIONAL DE VOILE	Association International des Ecoles de Voile
INTERNATIONALES SEGELHANDBUCH	Internationale Zeilscholen Vereniging
	Internationale Segelschulen-Vereinigung

Welcome to the sport of sailing!

The RYA Young Sailors' Scheme will help you to learn quickly, so that you can enjoy the sport more. Courses are run at hundreds of sailing schools, clubs, schools and other centres all over Britain, so you and your friends will never be far from a good place to sail.

We call it the Young Sailors' Scheme because it's not just for juniors under 12, nor for youth sailors over 13. Entry to the Scheme is open to *everyone* under the age of 16. Once you have started, you can stay in the Scheme until you have completed all the courses you need.

Once you have completed the Start Sailing courses and learnt to sail, the best way of getting more from the sport is to join a club. Most good dinghy sailing clubs have a junior or youth fleet, where you can make new friends and enjoy your sailing.

If the thrill of dinghy racing appeals, the Racing side of the RYA Young Sailors Scheme provides the perfect progression for you. The Red Badge course will prepare you for club racing, where you will be able to decide which of the many different dinghy classes is the one for you.

Club sailing might also give you more crewing practice. Although many sailing schools and centres use singlehanded dinghies so that you can learn to sail quickly, most of the popular dinghy classes are doublehanded boats. Club sailors are often short of crew, and besides getting some free sailing, you'll learn more about the sport if you want to progress to helming a dinghy.

Please don't think from this that crewing is a second-rate occupation; it covers

STUDENTS WITH SPECIAL NEEDS

Recognising that some students with disabilities or learning difficulties are unable to complete the full requirements for an RYA certificate without additional help, the scheme makes provision for certificates to be endorsed as appropriate. Please contact your nearest RYA dinghy centre or RYA HQ for more information.

a range of skills and good crews are sought after. The role of the racing crew is very important not only in trimming the jib and spinnaker, but in helping the helmsman decide on racing tactics.

As your racing skill develops, you will want to learn more about the sport to prepare yourself for open meetings and regattas in the class of your choice. That is where the White Badge course comes in, with courses usually being organised by the class associations or the RYA. After that, the Blue Badge course will prepare you for important national events.

If the challenge of independent dinghy sailing appeals more than racing, the Advanced Sailing side of the RYA Young Sailors' Scheme provides a structured series of courses to prepare you for day cruises, overnight dinghy camps or longer expeditions. Many of the traditional skills learnt, together with the background topics of meteorology and navigation, will be useful when you progress to sailing·in one of the "tall ships" or going cruising offshore.

As a young sailor, you'll find that your skills and knowledge are recognised within the Duke of Edinburgh's Award Scheme. All the courses outlined in this logbook can gain you points in the Physical Recreation section of the D of E Award, whilst the Advanced Sailing courses are designed to prepare you for expeditions afloat.

Finally, please remember that although the Young Sailors' Scheme has the twin branches of Racing and Advanced Sailing, there is nothing to stop you moving from one side to the other in order to learn more and enjoy both aspects of the sport.

Good sailing!

WHERE TO LEARN MORE

If you want to reach any of the Youth Class Associations, or the many organisations which provide sailing opportunities for young people, please contact the RYA at the address on p1. For details of schools' sailing in each of the home countries in the UK, please contact the following:

National School Sailing Association
Martyn Styles, Bellers Bush, Dover Road, Sandwich, Kent CT13 0DG

Northern Ireland Schools Sailing Association
Pat Quinn, 13 Woodview Crescent, Hillsborough Road, Lisburn, Co Down

Scottish Schools Sailing Association
RYA, Caledonia House, South Gyle, Edinburgh EH12 9DQ

Schools Sailing Association for Wales
Sandra Potts, WYA, 4 Lys y Mor, Plas Menai, Caernarfon, Gwynedd LL55 1UE

EQUIVALENT AWARDS

If you have completed courses within the training schemes run by the International Optimist Class Association or the National School Sailing Association, you qualify for equivalent awards in the RYA Young Sailors' Scheme. Please ask the Principal of your nearest RYA Recognised Teaching Establishment for the appropriate certificates.

RYA	IOCA	NSSA
Stage One	Grade One	Bronze
Stage Two	Grade Two	Silver
Stage Three	Grade Three	Gold
Racing - Red	Grade Four	
Racing - White	Grade Five	

TYPES OF BOAT USED FOR RYA YOUTH RACE TRAINING

Although sailing schools and centres will use a variety of suitable classes for basic training and an introduction to race training, the following classes are favoured for the higher levels of race training:

Singlehanders

Laser

Europe (girls) / Laser Radial

Topper

Optimist

Doublehanders

Laser 2 / 420

405

Cadet/Mirror

When deciding which type of boat to sail at a particular age, you must think carefully about your experience, weight, size and strength. If in doubt, ask your club race trainer or RYA coaching staff.

TO THE PARENTS OF VERY YOUNG SAILORS

GOING AFLOAT

It is always colder on water than it is ashore, and everyone who goes afloat should be warmly dressed. Children won't enjoy sailing if they are simply sitting shivering in the boat, so please encourage them to wear an extra sweater and a windproof jacket. They won't have much fun, either, if they keep slipping over in the boat, so non-slip, soft-soled shoes are useful.

Everyone who goes afloat in a dinghy should wear personal buoyancy, which will help in the unlikely event of capsize or falling out of the boat. Buoyancy aids are provided by all RYA recognised sailing schools, clubs and centres, but they are no use unless they are of the right size and properly fastened.

Anyone who goes dinghy sailing should be able to swim, just to show that they have confidence in the water. Nobody is expected to swim far, though, as the golden rule after capsize is to stay with the boat.

COURSE STRUCTURE

The RYA Young Sailors' Scheme has been designed to encourage children to start sailing within a sound framework of safety and tuition. No time limits are given for the different stages, as children learn at very different rates according to their age and enthusiasm. Instead, each of the early stages of the scheme are expressed in terms of competencies, giving instructors the flexibility to sign off each part of the syllabus as competence in that skill is demonstrated. When all the items for a particular stage are completed, the appropriate certificate may be issued by the Principal of the Recognised Teaching Establishment.

Sailing schools, clubs, schools and other centres vary widely in their course programmes, although all those which are RYA recognised will follow the RYA course syllabi given in this book. Some centres, for example, will provide hourly sessions over a long period, whilst others offer full-time residential courses.

If your child is learning at an RYA recognised teaching establishment, you should be reassured that tuition will be given in suitable, seaworthy dinghies by trained instructors, using supervision ratios appropriate to the location and the stage of instruction. Capsize recovery procedures will be conducted in a controlled way, with a suitable rescue boat in attendance.

COMPLETING THE LOGBOOK

The logbook section of this book provides a record of your child's sailing experience from the first time he goes afloat. Please ensure that every course he attends and all his own sailing is recorded in the Personal Log. If possible, get the authorisation signed by an instructor or sailing club official.

IF YOU HAVE RECEIVED A CERTIFICATE

FROM A TASTER SESSION, SUCH AS

AN RYA YOUNG OPPORTUNITY COURSE

OR AN ACIVITY HOLIDAY PROGRAMME,

PLEASE STICK IT HERE

START SAILING AWARDS

The aim of these awards is to provide an introduction to the sport of dinghy sailing in three easy steps. By the end of the three stages, you will be safety conscious and you will be able to sail a dinghy confidently in light winds.

START SAILING (STAGE ONE) AWARD

SECTION A:	PRACTICAL
By the end of the course, you should:	Be aware of wind direction Be able to put on personal buoyancy correctly (belt up and zip up!) Be confident in the water wearing personal buoyancy Be able to assist with rigging a dinghy Be able to cleat a halyard Be able to tie figure of eight and reef knots Be able to capsize and stay with the boat Be able to launch a dinghy and get under way with assistance Be a responsive crew under instruction* (i.e. adjust daggerboard, balance and foresail) Be able to steer and turn a dinghy when sailing (reach to reach) and when being towed Be able to paddle or row round a short triangular course (with sprit, paddle or oars) Be able to assist with recovery and stowage of dinghy and gear
SECTION B:	ONSHORE TEACHING
By the end of the course, you should:	Know what to wear for sailing (including footwear and headwear) Know the names of basic parts of a boat (i.e. hull, mast, rudder, tiller, centreboard, sheets etc) Know how to call for assistance Know how to prepare to be towed

*not applicable for singlehanders

SECTION A:	**PRACTICAL**

By the end of the course, you should:

Be able to rig a dinghy

Be able to tie a round turn and two half hitches and a bowline

Be able to get under way from, and return to, a beach or pontoon (offshore wind)

Be scooped in during capsize recovery*

Or be able to right a singlehanded dinghy

Be able to go about (close reach to close reach)

Be able to get out "of irons"

Be able to crew a dinghy effectively (i.e. adjust jib, centreboard and body weight)*

Be able to sail a figure of eight course across the wind under supervision

Be able to stop a dinghy by lying-to

Be aware of what is meant by a gybe

SECTION B:	**ONSHORE TEACHING**

By the end of the course, you should:

Know how to choose the right personal buoyancy

Know more ways of finding wind direction

Know what is meant by windward and leeward

Know how to prepare for a multiple tow

*not applicable to singlehanders

SECTION A:	PRACTICAL

By the end of the course, you should:	Be able to rig and launch without assistance in an onshore wind
	Be able to sail backwards away from pontoon in an offshore wind
	Be able to reef a dinghy ashore according to weather conditions
	Be able to right a capsized dinghy efficiently as helmsman/crew, bail out and sail on
	Be able to apply the basic rules of the road
	Be proficient at tacking and gybing and sail a figure of eight course upwind/downwind
	Be able to demonstrate all points of sailing
	Be able to apply the "five essentials"
	Be able to return to a beach, jetty or mooring safely

SECTION B:	ONSHORE TEACHING

By the end of the course, you should:	Know the points of sailing
	Know the basic rules of the road for sailing dinghies
	Know how to obtain a weather forecast
	Know when to reef
	Know what action to take to help those in distress

RACING AWARDS

RACING - RED BADGE

The aim of this award is to give a solid introduction to dinghy racing at club level. Although essentially a practical course, sessions afloat will be backed up by lectures and demonstrations ashore, and so there is some overlap between the two sections of the syllabus.

It is expected that every young sailor starting this course should be a competent helmsman or crew. For those who have not completed the Start Sailing part of the RYA scheme, this implies at least one full season's sailing.

SECTION A:	**PRACTICAL**
1. **Rigging**	Preparation of boat and equipment Boat tuning - centreboard, mast rake, kicker, cunningham, clew outhaul, traveller, barber haulers, mast ram
2. **Sailing techniques and manoeuvres**	The five essentials - sail setting, balance, trim, centreboard and course made good Roll tacking and gybing Tacking and gybing in strong winds Sailing to windward - telltales, clear wind Mark rounding - approach, other boats, rounding position Spinnaker handling (optional)
3. **Racing tactics**	Starting techniques - correct end, speed of approach Lee bow tactics Covering Finishing

SECTION B:	**ONSHORE TEACHING**
4. **Sailing theory and background**	Handicap v class racing Sailing Instructions Progress of a race from warning signal to finish Racing rules - fundamental rules, definitions, protests Insurance
5. **Meteorology**	Sources of information on major weather patterns Local weather patterns and strategy

RACING - WHITE BADGE

The aim of this award is to improve the techniques and knowledge of young club level sailors in preparation for open meetings and small regattas. Although essentially a practical course, sessions afloat will be backed up by lectures and demonstrations ashore, and so there is some overlap between the two sections of the syllabus.

It is expected that every young sailor starting this course should either have attended the RYA Red Badge racing course or have at least two full season's club racing experience, as helmsman or crew.

SECTION A: PRACTICAL

1. **Starting**	Use of transits Line bias evaluation Port or starboard end? Midline starts
2. **Tactics**	Attacking and defending a position Beating, reaching and running tactics
3. **Strategy**	Fastest course sailed - wind, current, waves and geography
4. **Boat handling and crew work**	Developed from Red Badge course
5. **Boat speed**	Tuning Effective use of rig controls to suit conditions Foils - position, shape and care Trim and balance
6. **Hiking - Trapeze techniques**	

SECTION B: ONSHORE TEACHING

7. **Open meeting preparation**

8. **Visual signals - Part II IYRR**

9. **Racing rules - Part IV IYRR**

10. **Protest procedures - Part VI IYRR**

RACING - BLUE BADGE

The aim of this award is to improve the racing skills and knowledge of experienced young club racers and open meeting sailors in preparation for important national events. Although essentially a practical course, sessions afloat will be backed up by lectures and demonstrations ashore, and so there is some overlap between the two sections of the syllabus.

It is expected that every young sailor starting this course should have attended Red and White Badge racing courses or have at least three full seasons' racing experience, as helmsman or crew.

SECTION A:	PRACTICAL
1. **Boat handling skills**	Developed from Red and White Badge courses Tacking, gybing, spinnaker hoist and drop Boat characteristics
2. **Compass work**	Use for starts Windshifts, windbends and tracking Tactical use
3. **Starting techniques**	Port tack approaches Port end going left or right up the beat Starboard end going left or right up the beat Transits - starting in middle of line Gate starts
4. **Tactics**	Boat to boat, boat to group, boat to fleet Racing in large fleets Upwind - speed made good Downwind - gybing angles

SECTION B: ONSHORE TEACHING

5.	**Self preparation**	Physical and mental
6.	**Boat preparation**	Hull finish, fittings, spars, sails, legality, certificate
7.	**Boat tuning**	All controls, calibration, evaluation, recording
8.	**Strategy**	Land masses, tide/current, gradient wind, surface wind, which way to go
9.	**Racing rules**	Fundamental Rules, Definitions, Rules 1-78 and 79.1
10.	**Meteorology**	Weather systems Effects related to race area Weather forecasts and interpretation

ADVANCED SAILING AWARDS

ADVANCED SAILING - RED AWARD

The aim of this award is to develop the basic skills of dinghy sailing in order to sail more efficiently. It is expected that every young sailor starting this course has already mastered the skills of the Start Sailing, Stage 3 course or equivalent. In practical terms, this implies a season's sailing between courses.

SECTION A:	PRACTICAL
By the end of the course, you should:	Be able to demonstrate the five essentials in a sailing dinghy Be able to communicate as helmsman or crew * Be able to roll tack Be able to use telltales for sail trim Be able to take advantage of windshifts Be able to roll gybe Be able to tack and gybe in stronger winds Be able to tie a sheet bend and clove hitch Be able to recover an inverted dinghy and sail on (if water depth allows) Be able to round marks/buoys efficiently Be able to hoist/set/gybe/lower a spinnaker (if available)* Be able to participate in a half-day cruise (picnic)

SECTION B:	ONSHORE TEACHING
By the end of the course, you should:	Know how to find information about inland sailing - byelaws and permits Know the dangers of overhead power lines, locks & weirs Know how to give expired air resuscitation Know how to stop bleeding Know how to treat shock Know the signs of hypothermia and how to treat it

SECTION C:	COASTAL (Optional)
By the end of the course, you should:	Be able to apply Section A on tidal waters Be able to use transits Know basic tidal theory - Ebb and flow, springs and neaps Know how to use tide tables Know how to find the direction of tidal streams Know how to use a compass to take bearings Know the meanings of IALA buoys

*not applicable to singlehanders

The aim of this award is to cover the traditional skills of boat handling and seamanship in preparation for more independent sailing. It is expected that every young sailor starting this course will already have mastered the practical skills and absorbed the background knowledge of the Advanced Sailing - Red Badge course. In practical terms, this implies a season's sailing between courses.

SECTION A:	PRACTICAL
By the end of the course, you should:	Be able to rig a dinghy using all the boat's normal equipment Be able to tie a rolling hitch and fisherman's bend Be able to make a common whipping and an eye splice Be able to leave and return to a jetty or mooring Be able to leave and return to a windward & leeward shore Be able to anchor a dinghy* Be able to heave to and reef afloat* Be able to prepare a dinghy to be towed Be able to tow another sailing dinghy Be able to recover a man overboard Be able to apply the Collision Regulations in a dinghy Be able to plan, prepare & participate in a half-day cruise

SECTION B:	ONSHORE TEACHING
By the end of the course, you should:	Know how to obtain weather information Know what is meant by the Beaufort Scale Know the main characteristics of high and low pressure areas Know the significance of major changes in barometric pressure Know the basis of how to interpret a synoptic chart

SECTION C:	COASTAL (Optional)
By the end of the course, you should:	Be able to apply Section A on tidal waters Be able to steer a compass course Be able to apply variation and deviation Be able to fix your position Have a basic understanding of charts & important symbols Know the effect of wind with/against tidal stream

*not applicable to singlehanders

The aim of this award is to provide the practical skills and background knowledge needed for independent dinghy sailing. By the end of the course, the successful sailor should have a confident, safe, seamanlike approach to sailing and will be capable of handling a sailing dinghy in strong wind conditions.

It is expected that every young sailor starting the course has mastered the practical skills and background knowledge of the Advanced Sailing - White Badge course. In practical terms, this implies a season's sailing between courses.

The practical skills covered in this course are similar to those used as the basis of the pre-entry assessment for potential RYA Dinghy Instructors. Anyone planning to train as an Instructor should ensure that they have these skills and the accompanying background knowledge.

SECTION A:	**PRACTICAL**
By the end of the course, you should:	Be able to sail in a variety of wind conditions to a high standard using all the boat's equipment to best advantage, including the following tasks:
	Beating, reaching and running
	Heaving to and reefing afloat
	Man overboard recovery
	Launching and recovery, including lee shores
	Sailing backwards
	Sailing a tight circular course
	Anchoring/ mooring/ coming alongside
	Righting a capsized dinghy
	Use of spinnaker and trapeze
	Boat handling in adverse circumstances:
	Sailing without a centreboard
	Sailing without a rudder
	Towing another sailing dinghy
	Be able to plan, prepare and participate in a full day cruise (with overnight camp if possible)

SECTION B: ONSHORE TEACHING

By the end of the course, you should:

Know the names and uses of sail and mast controls

Know the basic principles of dinghy construction - grp, plywood, plastic, traditional wooden hulls

Know the principles of dinghy and equipment maintenance

Know how to make emergency repairs to hulls and equipment

Know how to interpret shipping forecasts

Know how local weather patterns might influence forecasts

SECTION C: COASTAL (Optional)

By the end of the course, you should:

Be able to apply Section A on tidal waters

Be able to demonstrate knowledge of the onshore and coastal sections of the Red and White Badge syllabi

Be able to plan and prepare for an overnight dinghy cruise/camp, including route, alternatives and refuges; preparation of clothing, boat, equipment and food

Know how to use sources of navigational information - charts, tidal stream atlases, nautical almanacs

Know how to calculate tidal heights

Know how to fix position by transits and/or bearings

Know the principles of dead reckoning

Know how to establish a course to steer

Know the limitations of chartwork in a dinghy

Know how to keep a log

PERSONAL LOG

Date	Class/Boat	Activity (eg Leisure, Racing, Course)	Authenticating Signature

RECORD OF ACHIEVEMENT - NOTES FOR PARENTS

Records of Achievement are widely used in schools as a means of reporting progress and highlighting what has been learnt. The page overleaf will allow students to integrate what they have learnt through sailing with other aspects of their school development.

Remember that even though a sailing course may have been organised and run at a sailing club or youth-based organisation, this record - properly completed - will still be valid as a contribution to the student's Record of Achievement.

The record can contribute to the end-of-school career (Year 11) Record of Achievement; RYA certificates may be used as supporting documentary evidence, and special versions of the different awards within the Young Sailors' Scheme suitable for RoA presentation are available from RYA recognised teaching establishments.

It has been widely recognised in Outdoor Education for many years that sailing has the potential to offer educational values far beyond any hard skills which may have been learnt. The experience of a sailing course, particularly if it involves a residential element, can provide a strong medium for personal and social development through the challenge of the environment.

Closer to school, imaginative teachers have used sailing as a vehicle to deliver many aspects of the curriculum, from the obvious topics within applied mathematics and physics to aspects of botany, history, sociology and music.

National School Sailing Association

ROYAL YACHTING ASSOCIATION

RECORD OF ACHIEVEMENT - DINGHY SAILING

Student's Comments

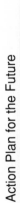

Action Plan for the Future

ROYAL YACHTING ASSOCIATION

RYA MEMBERSHIP APPLICATION FORM

Personal
Membership
costs very little
and means
a great deal . . .

RYA

the national voice.

Who can join?

ANYONE who enjoys going afloat whether by sail or power. You may be a beginner or a weekend club enthusiast, an Olympic hopeful or an Admiral's Cup competitor, a serious blue water explorer or a round the world yacht racer. The RYA is open to everyone.

Is it different from a Yacht club?

Yes. The RYA is a national membership organisation providing a range of services and benefits that are different to those available from clubs. However, many RYA members also belong to a club of their choice.

Why join?

Being a member of the RYA means that you can:

- use the expert legal, cruising, racing and windsurfing advice services when you need them
- obtain up-to-date information on training, moorings, navigation and foreign cruising procedures
- help the RYA protect its members' activities from outside interference and unnecessary bureaucracy
- make use of the special RYA restaurant and lounge at selected boat shows
- benefit from the free offers and discounts available

What free offers are available to RYA members?

- A Helmsman's Overseas Certificate of Competence (useful for those who cruise abroad)
- Allocation of a sail number
- Two RYA publications a year, (choose from a whole range of subjects), a book token worth £5.00 (on books from the RYA catalogue) or an RYA diary
- Quarterly magazine delivered to your home
- RYA Visa Card (no annual fee, application subject to status)

Windsurfing members only, receive third party insurance and one RYA publication

r book token worth £2.50)

nior members receive one free RYA
blication (worth £2.50) and a
ndsurfing junior member receives the
ird party insurance only.

ow about discounts?

10% (or more depending on
qualifications) reduction on Yacht
Insurance arranged through the RYA
Brokers Bishop Skinner and Co. Ltd.
20% reduction on Car Rental through
Europcar Interrent
40% possible reduction on premiums
with the Hospital and Medical
Care Association
Reduction on measurement certificate
fees

Vill my membership
nake a difference?

es. With every new member the RYA
trengthens its voice to speak up and
epresent the interests of individuals –
eople like you who go afloat in their spare
me. Not everyone views boating in quite
he same way as RYA members. Pressure
rom other organisations such as the EC,
he port authorities, the environmental
bby and the foreshore landowners can
ffect your freedom afloat.

OUR MEMBERSHIP MATTERS.

How can I make my voice heard?

Write to the RYA expressing your opinions
and attend the RYA AGM. It is a democratic
organisation and your views are important.

How much does it cost?

An adult personal member £16
(£15 by direct debit).
A young person (under 21) £8

MEMBERSHIP APPLICATION FORM

My principal boating interest is: (tick 1 box only)

Powerboat Racing ☐   Sail Racing ☐   Sail Cruising ☐   Motor Cruising ☐   Windsurfing ☐

PLEASE USE BLOCK CAPITALS

NAME
Mr/Mrs/Miss

Address

Postcode

Type of Membership Required (tick as applicable)

☐ **Personal** £16 (£15 if you pay by Direct Debit).

☐ **Student** £8   18 to 21

☐ **Junior under 18** £8

Student & Junior Date of Birth _____

Signed

THE EASY WAY TO PAY   Originators identification number: 955213

DIRECT Debit

INSTRUCTIONS TO YOUR BANK OR BUILDING SOCIETY TO PAY DIRECT DEBITS

Please complete parts 1 to 5 to instruct your bank or building society to make payments directly from your account.
Then return the form to: **Royal Yachting Association, RYA House, Romsey Road, Eastleigh, Hants SO50 9YA**

1. **Name of Account Holder**

2. **Account number**

3. **Sort code** ☐☐ — ☐☐ — ☐☐

4. **Please write the full postal address of your bank or building society branch in the box below**

To: The Manager

Postcode

Banks or Building Society may refuse to accept instructions to pay
Direct Debits from some types of account.

5. **Your instructions to the bank or building society and signature.**

* I instruct you to pay Direct Debits from my account at the request of the Royal Yachting Association.
* The amounts are variable and are to be debited on various dates.
* I understand that the Royal Yachting Association may change the amounts and dates only after giving me prior notice.
* I will inform the bank or building society in writing if I wish to cancel these instructions.
* I understand that if any Direct Debit is paid which breaks the terms of the instruction, the bank or building society will make a refund.

Signature(s):

Date:

Cash, Cheque, Postal Order

enclosed for   £ _____   Made payable to the
Royal Yachting Association

077

Office Use only: Membership No. Allocated

Office use/Centre Stamp:

Comments by sailing instructor/teacher/supporting adult

HOW TO USE THE RECORD OF ACHIEVEMENT

1/ Use the Comments column in the Personal Log throughout your sailing as a diary to record your experience.

2/ When you want to enter your recent experience in your Record of Achievement, remove this centre page from the logbook and copy it.

3/ Using the photocopy, complete the student comment box and action plan.

4/ Give the copy to your course leader and discuss it with him.

5/ The course leader will add his comments and discuss them.

6/ When both you and the course leader agree that the Record of Achievement is a fair assessment, the comments can be transferred to this master copy.

7/ Finally, you should return the master copy to your school tutor or form teacher.

8/ If you want to complete another Record of Achievement at a later date, spare copies of this pull-out are available from your teaching establishment, the NSSA or the RYA.

9/ The Record of Achievement is enhanced by other evidence, such as certificates, reports or awards gained at activities and events you have attended.

10/ If you want a more formal A4 certificate to include in your Record of Achievement wallet instead of the normal RYA proficiency certificates, contact your teaching establishment, the NSSA or the RYA.

Comments
(eg Location, weather, helming or crewing, what you achieved, what you learnt)

PERSONAL LOG

Date	Class/Boat	Activity *(eg Leisure, Racing, Course)*	Authenticating Signature

Comments
(eg Location, weather, helming or crewing, what you achieved, what you learnt)

PERSONAL LOG

Date	Class/Boat	Activity *(eg Leisure, Racing, Course)*	Authenticating Signature

Comments
(eg Location, weather, helming or crewing, what you achieved, what you learnt)

CERTIFICATE CHECK LISTS FOR INDIVIDUAL ITEMS

The check lists below allow you to record your progress through the RYA Young Sailors' Scheme. Your instructor will sign off each item as you show you have completed it. When all the items for a particular stage are signed off, the certificate or sticker can be issued. Don't forget to record all your courses and your own sailing in the Personal Log (pp18–23).

START SAILING - STAGE ONE

The student is: Instructor's signature

Aware of wind direction   ....

Able to put on personal buoyancy correctly   ....

Confident in the water wearing personal
    buoyancy   ....

Able to assist with rigging a dinghy   ....

Able to capsize and stay with the boat   ....

Able to launch a dinghy and get under way
    with assistance   ....

A responsive crew under instruction*   ....

Able to steer and turn a dinghy when sailing
    and being towed   ....

Able to paddle or row round a short
    triangular course   ....

Able to assist with recovery and stowage   ....

The student knows:

What to wear for sailing   ....

The names of basic parts of a boat   ....

How to call for assistance   ....

How to prepare to be towed   ....

*not singlehanders

PLEASE STICK YOUR RYA

START SAILING STAGE ONE

CERTIFICATE HERE

Please note that no record of Dinghy Proficiency
certificates is kept by the RYA. Enquiries about
lost certificates should be made to the centre
where you took the course

START SAILING - STAGE TWO

The student has:	Instructor's signature
Rigged a dinghy	....
Tied a round turn and two half hitches and a bowline	....
Got under way from, and returned to, a beach or pontoon (offshore wind)	....
Been scooped in during capsize recovery *Or* righted a singlehanded dinghy	....
Gone about (close reach to close reach)	....
Got out "of irons"	....
Crewed a dinghy effectively*	....
Sailed a figure of eight course across the wind under supervision	....
Stopped a dinghy by lying-to	....

The student knows:

What is meant by a gybe	....
How to choose the right personal buoyancy	....
More ways of finding wind direction	....
What is meant by windward and leeward	....
How to prepare for a multiple tow	....

*not singlehanders

26

PLEASE STICK YOUR RYA

START SAILING STAGE TWO

CERTIFICATE HERE

Please note that no record of Dinghy Proficiency
certificates is kept by the RYA. Enquiries about
lost certificates should be made to the centre
where you took the course

START SAILING - STAGE THREE

The student has: Instructor's signature

Rigged and launched without assistance in
    an onshore wind   ....

Sailed backwards away from a pontoon in an
    offshore wind   ....

Reefed a dinghy ashore according to
    weather conditions   ....

Righted a capsized dinghy efficiently as
    helmsman/crew   ....

Applied the basic rules of the road   ....

Tacked and gybed proficiently   ....

Sailed a figure of eight course upwind/
    downwind   ....

Demonstrated all points of sailing   ....

Applied the "five essentials"   ....

Returned to a beach, jetty or mooring safely   ....

The student knows:

The points of sailing   ....

The basic rules of the road for sailing
    dinghies   ....

How to obtain a weather forecast   ....

When to reef   ....

What action to take to help those in distress   ....

PLEASE STICK YOUR RYA

START SAILING STAGE THREE

CERTIFICATE HERE

If you have completed the NSSA
badge scheme, please stick your
NSSA record card here instead

Please note that no record of Dinghy Proficiency
certificates is kept by the RYA. Enquiries about
lost certificates should be made to the centre
where you took the course

ADVANCED SAILING - RED BADGE

The student has: Instructor's signature

Demonstrated the five essentials   ....

Communicated as helmsman or crew   ....

Roll tacked and roll gybed effectively   ....

Used telltales for sail trim   ....

Shown ability to take advantage of windshifts ....

Shown ability to tack/gybe in stronger winds   ....

Tied a sheet bend and clove hitch   ....

Rounded marks/buoys efficiently   ....

Participated in a half-day cruise (picnic) ....

(Optional items if possible)

Recovered an inverted dinghy   ....

Hoisted/set/gybed/lowered a spinnaker   ....
    (if available)

The student knows:

How to find information about inland sailing   ....

The dangers of overhead power lines, locks
    and weirs   ....

How to give expired air resuscitation   ....

How to stop bleeding   ....

How to treat shock   ....

The signs of hypothermia and how to treat it   ....

30

COASTAL (Optional)

The student: Instructor's signature

Is able to apply Section A on tidal waters   ....

Is able to use transits   ....

Knows basic tidal theory   ....

Knows how to use tide tables   ....

Knows how to find the direction of tidal streams   ....

Knows how to use a compass to take bearings   ....

Knows the meanings of IALA buoys   ....

PLEASE STICK YOUR RYA

ADVANCED SAILING RED BADGE

STICKER HERE

ADVANCED SAILING - WHITE BADGE

The student has: Instructor's signature

Rigged a dinghy using all the boat's normal
equipment   ....

Tied a rolling hitch and fisherman's bend   ....

Made a common whipping and an eye splice   ....

Left and returned to a jetty or mooring   ....

Left and returned to a windward & leeward
shore   ....

Anchored a dinghy   ....

Heaved to and reefed afloat   ....

Prepared a dinghy to be towed   ....

Towed another sailing dinghy   ....

Recovered a man overboard   ....

Applied the IRPCS in a sailing dinghy   ....

Planned, prepared and participated in a
half-day cruise   ....

The student knows:

How to obtain weather information   ....

What is meant by the Beaufort Scale   ....

The main characteristics of high and low
pressure areas   ....

The significance of major changes in
barometric pressure   ....

The basis of how to interpret a synoptic chart   ....

COASTAL (Optional)

The student:

Instructor's signature

Is able to apply Section A on tidal waters

....

Is able to steer a compass course

....

Is able to apply variation and deviation

....

Is able to fix a position

....

Has a basic understanding of charts and
    symbols

....

Knows the effect of wind with/against tidal
    stream

....

PLEASE STICK YOUR RYA

ADVANCED SAILING WHITE BADGE

STICKER HERE

ADVANCED SAILING -BLUE BADGE

The student has: Instructor's signature

Sailed to a high standard using all the
    boat's equipment to best advantage   ....

Planned, prepared and participated in a day
    cruise   ....

The student knows:

The names and uses of sail and mast
    controls   ....

The basic principles of dinghy construction   ....

The principles of maintenance   ....

How to make emergency repairs   ....

How to interpret shipping forecasts   ....

How local weather patterns might influence   ....
    forecasts

COASTAL (Optional)

The student:

Is able to apply Section A on tidal waters   ....

Is able to demonstrate knowledge of the
    onshore and coastal sections of the Red   ....
    and White Badge syllabi

Is able to plan and prepare for a dinghy   ....
    cruise/camp

Knows how to use sources of navigational   ....
    information

Knows how to calculate tidal heights   ....

Knows how to fix position by transits and/or
    bearings   ....

Knows the principles of dead reckoning   ....

Knows how to establish a course to steer   ....

Knows the limitations of chartwork in a
    dinghy   ....

Knows how to keep a log   ....

PLEASE STICK YOUR RYA

ADVANCED SAILING BLUE BADGE

STICKER HERE

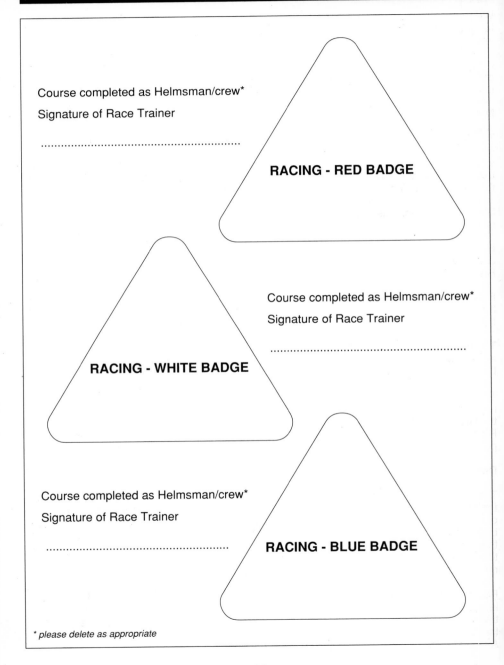

PLEASE STICK YOUR RACING BADGES HERE

Course completed as Helmsman/crew*

Signature of Race Trainer

....

RACING - RED BADGE

Course completed as Helmsman/crew*

Signature of Race Trainer

....

RACING - WHITE BADGE

Course completed as Helmsman/crew*

Signature of Race Trainer

....

RACING - BLUE BADGE

* please delete as appropriate

36